OUT OF THE MOUTHS OF

A 31-Day Devotional for Moms

Lessons from Little Ones
in Everyday Life

NICOLE B. BARNETT

Rewards
Publishing

Out of the Mouths of Babes, A 31-Day Devotional for Moms:
Lessons from Little Ones in Everyday Life

Visit the author's website at www.yourmommymoments.com.

Scripture quotations marked (CSB) are taken from the Christian Standard Bible®, Copyright © 2017 by Holman Bible Publishers. Used by permission. Christian Standard Bible®, and CSB® are federally registered trademarks of Holman Bible Publishers.

Scripture quotations marked as (GNT) are taken from the Good News Translation in Today's English Version - Second Edition © 1992 by American Bible Society. Used by permission.

Scripture quotations marked (NLT) are taken from the Holy Bible, New Living Translation, copyright ©1996, 2004, 2015 by Tyndale House Foundation. Used by permission of Tyndale House Publishers, a Division of Tyndale House Ministries, Carol Stream, Illinois 60188. All rights reserved.

Scripture quotations marked (NIV) are taken from the Holy Bible, New International Version®, NIV®. Copyright © 1973, 1978, 1984, 2011 by Biblica, Inc.™ Used by permission of Zondervan. All rights reserved worldwide. www.zondervan.com The "NIV" and "New International Version" are trademarks registered in the United States Patent and Trademark Office by Biblica, Inc.™

Scripture quotations marked (NIrV) are taken from the Holy Bible, New International Reader's Version®, NIrV® Copyright © 1995, 1996, 1998, 2014 by Biblica, Inc.™ Used by permission of Zondervan. All rights reserved worldwide. www.zondervan.com. The "NIrV" and "New International Reader's Version" are trademarks registered in the United States Patent and Trademark Office by Biblica, Inc.™

Scripture quotations marked (NKJV) are taken from the New King James Version®. Copyright © 1982 by Thomas Nelson. Used by permission. All rights reserved.

Cover design by Creative Encouragement
Cover enhancement by Remi Bryant

Interior design by Sandra Jurca

LCCN: 2020917490
Print ISBN: 978-1-7355846-0-7
eBook ISBN: 978-1-7355846-1-4

Rewards Publishing
Upper Marlboro, MD

This devotional is dedicated to:

*Imperfect moms like me who press forward
every single day. You truly make a difference
with everything you do.*

*Jeff, Karis, Naomi & Joy.
I wouldn't trade our family adventure
together for anything.
You make being a wife and mom so worth it.*

Acknowledgements

I truly thank God for gracing me with an incredible husband and three precious rewards (Psalm 127:3).

To *my mother, Anita Reid Boseman,* for encouraging me to write down every story I shared about her grandbabies.

To *Endelea,* for loving my three girls and helping me care for them through the most challenging time of my life.

To *Tina* for your friendship, continuous encouragement to "just write," and countless hours of time to edit my initial manuscript.

To *Lisa, Regina, Jualecia, Vanessa, Teresa, and Mom Barnett* for sharing your mommy-moment stories.

To *Elisa and Jualecia*, for your friendship and enduring extremely rough drafts of these devotions.

To *Donna, Celeste, Robin, Sandy, Tiffany Nicole, and Remi,* for your guidance, expertise, and encouragement along the publishing journey. You ladies are a blessing.

Table of Contents

Introduction

As a mom juggling a newborn, toddler, and preschooler at home, my definition of a "successful day" was comprised of only *two* things. One, the house didn't burn down. Two, everyone (including me) still had ten fingers and ten toes by the end of the night! Those two accomplishments were about all I could manage during that season of life. *Can any mom out there relate?*

Fast forward a few years and a sobering reality slowly set in: my children were teaching *me* much more than I was teaching them. God had a way of taking everyday exchanges and conversations with my kids—simple "mommy-moments"—and translating them into divine messages from Him. Sometimes the messages inspired and encouraged me, while other times I felt convicted and challenged. But there was no doubt God was speaking through my children. I just needed to listen.

This devotional reveals adventures of everyday life with my kids, along with a few tales other moms have graciously shared about their children. Through these stories, my hope is for you to be encouraged on this sometimes wild and crazy journey of motherhood. I also hope you begin to embrace a simple truth: our children can bring us precious God-moments, even within all the craziness.

Over the next 31 days, begin experiencing God through a different lens: your ordinary encounters with children—especially the very ones God has *gifted* specifically to you.

I challenge you to listen to your children with a different ear. You might be surprised at the messages God is trying to reveal. Messages that draw you closer to His heart and His Word. Messages *"out of the mouths of babes."* (Psalm 8:2)

Day 1

Maintain Perspective

*M*ixing toddlers with family devotions sounds like a recipe for disaster, right? Yet adding a pinch of sheer will, a dash of determination, and a heaping tablespoon of humor can result in some sweet family memories. Our daughters were around ages six, four, and two when my husband began sharing short Bible stories and lessons with us as a family. These few minutes sometimes ranged from being an exercise in frustration to outright amusing, but we earned an "A" for effort.

I especially remember one devotional time when our girls were a little older, ages eight, six, and four. They listened attentively as their dad shared about *spiritual adoption.* In fact, they were quite curious about this notion of being adopted into the family of God by accepting Christ into their hearts. The girls asked probing questions as only little kids can. And they seemed to be catching on to the concept of God graciously adopting us as His children . . . or so I thought.

Just a few minutes after the lesson, I tried to get my two younger daughters to say the word *adoption.* None of my subtle hints were leading them to state the right answer. Exasperated, I pleaded, "Think! What do you call it when a husband and wife take in a child who wasn't born to them, but they raise the child like it was theirs all along?" Six-year-old Naomi contemplated my question for a few seconds, then emphatically answered: "Kidnapping!"

Okay . . . so that wasn't the word I was going for, but I could certainly appreciate her perspective.

Even though we are indeed lovingly adopted by our Heavenly Father, don't we sometimes behave more like we've been kidnapped by God? Instead of appreciating all the provision and kindness from our Father, we complain about what is or isn't happening in our lives. Or we spend most of our prayer time asking God to meet our needs and desires, and very little time thanking Him just for who He is. God has graciously adopted us into His family. Yet we sometimes run away from home in rebellion and disobedience. Or we struggle against God as if we're being held against our wills by a kidnapper.

I confess, it's challenging to keep a grateful attitude consistently. Selfishness and entitlement creep in out of nowhere. Our problems, needs, and desires are real, and they can easily consume us. But if we re-focus our hearts on the amazing gift we have in the God of the universe *choosing* to become our Father, ungratefulness begins to fade away.

Do you usually have the perspective of a grateful adopted child who has a loving Heavenly Father? Or would you more likely be described as a complaining child of the King? Let's commit to a heart of gratitude each day for the blessing of simply being adopted into the family of God.

God decided in advance to adopt us into his own family by bringing us to himself through Jesus Christ. This is what he wanted to do, and it gave him great pleasure.

EPHESIANS 1:5 (NLT)

I will give thanks to you, Lord, with all my heart; I will tell of all your wonderful deeds. PSALM 9:1 (NIV)

Think it Through: What specific challenge or trial are you facing right now? Determine how you can have a grateful attitude in your circumstance, simply because you are a child of the King.

Make it Personal: God, thank You for adopting me into Your family. Keep me mindful of all I have to be grateful for, no matter what challenges I face. Today, I am grateful for:

_____

_____

_____

_____

_____

Day 2

✎

Hall of Faith

The dark, lengthy hallway in my parents' home was not looking very appealing to four-year-old Joy. Her desired destination was the bathroom, but to reach it she would have to navigate her way down a path she dreaded. *"Ple-e-e-ease* come with me Mommy!" she begged, clinging to my leg. My initial thought was to encourage my preschooler to make the trip alone; to face her fears and grow towards more independence. However, I ultimately decided to escort Joy down the hall and at least turn on the lights along the way.

As she clasped my hand and we took our first steps, I reminded Joy that she never has to be afraid because

God is always with her. Joy smiled up at me and replied, "Oh Mommy, I know that God is always with me. But right now, I need someone I can *see*!"

Can you relate? I certainly can. Like my daughter, I know that God is always with me and there for me. Yet I have a tendency to place my faith in "real live people" for that immediate sense of understanding, reassurance, or security when I need it. Depending on the situation, I might look to my husband, my sister, a friend, or a mentor. There's something about having a flesh-and-blood person to rely on in a time of distress or uncertainty.

Maybe finding solace in a fellow human isn't your tendency. Perhaps you look to food for comfort, money for stability, movies or music for escape—anything that gives an immediate sense of feeling better or at least provides a distraction. In essence, we more readily seek out other people or things for temporary fixes to distress instead of looking to God.

We have countless opportunities to lay every concern we face before the One who holds the ultimate solutions to all of our circumstances. It's up to us to go to God first for wisdom and resist that inclination to turn to other seemingly instant sources for help, assurance or answers.

We exercise our faith when we pause to seek God and then follow His leading. Like a muscle, our faith grows stronger when we stretch to use it in unfamiliar ways. As we experience God building a track record of His faithfulness in our lives, we become more apt to seek and rely on Him first in all things. And who better to turn to than our Heavenly Father?

Struggles will indeed arise from day to day. Parenting struggles, marriage struggles, financial struggles, job struggles, health struggles, and on and on. In each situation, take a moment to ask yourself, "Am I putting more faith in what I can see, or *Who* I can't see?" Then exercise your faith by putting your trust in the Master of the universe.

Faith is being sure of what we hope for. It is being sure of what we do not see.   HEBREWS 11:1 (NIRV)

Without faith it is impossible to please God . . . he rewards those who look to him.   HEBREWS 11:6 (NIRV)

Think it Through: What current situation in your life is causing you concern, worry, or fear? Commit or re-commit to placing your faith in God to see you through, no matter how challenging the circumstances may seem.

Make it Personal: Lord, let me place my faith in You and You alone. Help me to remember that without faith, it is impossible to please You. Today, I fully trust You with:

_____

_____

_____

_____

_____

Day 3

A Way Out

While pregnant with her second child, Regina's three-year-old son DeeJay was thrilled about becoming a big brother. He was hoping for a baby sister, and he often sang and talked to his in-utero sibling. About seven months into Regina's pregnancy, DeeJay crawled into his mom's lap and looked perplexed as he rubbed her protruding belly. He wiggled around as if he was searching for something and eventually made his way up to his mom's face. He carefully pried her lips open with his curious fingers, then looked skeptically inside her mouth and asked, "*How* is the baby going to come out Mommy?"

Regina could only laugh as she assured her son, "Not *that* way little one—definitely not that way!"

Can you relate to little DeeJay? Sometimes we find ourselves in situations where we just can't see how things are going to work out, turn out, or come out. *How am I going handle yet another project at work? Is my marriage ever going to change? What if this is the wrong school for my child? Is my father going to recover from cancer? Will we have enough money to pay the bills this month? How will I ever reconcile with my friend?* The questions go on and on.

Our worry lists can be never-ending, and I should know. I'm a recovering worry-aholic. With God's grace, I've made progress over the years in learning to guard my mind against worry. However, it is still my natural predisposition to worry about the past, present, and future; about big things, little things, and in-between things; about anything and everything.

I've learned a few things over the years about worrying. One, whenever I try to determine exactly how God is going to work out a troubling situation, the solution *never* unfolds the way I envision. Two, whenever I worry, the detrimental conclusions I concoct in my brain are never as bad as the actual outcome. And three, the time and energy I spend worrying could be so much better spent elsewhere in my life.

Even with all I have learned, "not worrying" is a concept that still manages to elude me at times. However, Philippians 4:6 provides these critical instructions:

Do not be anxious about anything,
but in every situation, by prayer and petition,
with thanksgiving, present your requests to God. (NIV)

So what's the strategy? Pray, don't worry. *Pray, don't worry.* It sounds simple enough, but it's often extremely difficult to do. The key is catching our thoughts when they start to drift towards worrying. Once we are aware of this drift, we can call to mind God's Word, His character, and His very nature.

Isaiah 55:8 reminds us that God's thoughts are not like our thoughts. It seems obvious, but it's challenging to truly embrace that God is not only more than capable of working things out, but eventually working things out *for our good* (Romans 8:28). He's God. Nothing is impossible for Him (Matthew 19:26).

Does that make us immune to the pain, hardships, and difficulties of life? Not at all. But we can *choose* to rest in God's hands. No matter how many times we have to keep making that choice, it is a choice we can make.

Yes, we can choose not to worry. We can choose to trust God to work things out, to protect us, guide us, and provide for us every step of the way—no matter the outcome. He's already got it figured out, so leave it in His sovereign hands to work out.

Cast all your anxiety on him because he cares for you.

1 PETER 5:7 (NIV)

Jesus looked at them and said, "With man this is impossible, but with God all things are possible." MATTHEW 19:26 (CSB)

Think it Through: What worries do you have today? Make a list leaving space under each item. Write a one-sentence prayer for each worry, then cross each worry off the list.

Make it Personal: Lord, help me follow 1 Peter 5:7 and truly cast my cares on You. Whenever I begin to worry, help me stop and pray to You with confidence. Allow my heart to rest safely in You. Give me Your peace when I am feeling anxious. Teach me to receive Your gift of being able to pray and not worry. Today I place the following concern into Your hands:

_____

_____

_____

_____

_____

Day 4

Minding My Own Prayers

This is embarrassing to admit, but confession is good for the soul, right? When my children were first learning to pray as toddlers, sometimes I actually *corrected* their prayers. It seemed like a spiritual mommy-thing to do at the time; in retrospect, not so spiritual.

Four-year-old Joy would pray, "God, we thank You for Your *glo-o-o-ry*, and for Your *so-o-o--ul*, and for Your thanks." I could understand thanking God for His glory, but thanking God for His soul and His thanks just didn't *sound* right. So, like a self-appointed prayer theologian, I would attempt to correct the heartfelt prayers of a child.

Sounds a bit insane, right? I do have a role as a mom to help teach my children to pray. But in this case, I was more concerned about the "technicalities" of my daughter's prayers instead of acknowledging the sincerity of her heart. Joy wasn't praying *to* me or *for* me anyway!

Instead of being so determined to edit my child's prayers, perhaps I should have been assessing my own prayer life. We can all use a prayer self-checkup from time to time. A good place to start might be to ask a few questions:

- *How sincere or heartfelt are my prayers?*
- *Do I repeat familiar phrases, or do I earnestly pour out my heart to God with humility?*
- *Do I whiz through the list of things I need God to do for me? Or do I come seeking to spend time with Him and hear His voice?*
- *Do I hesitate or avoid praying because I'm not sure of what to say or how to say it?*

I am utterly convinced that we should ask God to give us hearts to pray like our children; to be candid and not worry about the right words or how it sounds; to trust that our Heavenly Father clearly sees and knows our hearts. He takes great delight in our desire to have genuine conversations with Him.

Jesus said, "Let the little children come to me. Don't keep them away. The kingdom of heaven belongs to people like them." MATTHEW 19:14 (NIrV)

In the same way, the Holy Spirit helps us when we are weak. We don't know what we should pray for. But the Spirit himself prays for us. He prays through groans too deep for words. ROMANS 8:26 (NIrV)

Think it Through: How would you describe your prayer time with God? Meaningful? Predictable? Fulfilling? Pointless? Insightful? Confusing? Comforting? What might help make your personal time with Him more meaningful? Try journaling your prayers.

Make it Personal: Lord, help me come to You openly and honestly like a child. I want to pray with a sincere heart and listen to Your voice. Help me spend time in Your presence seeking Your face, and finding comfort and rest in Your arms. Today I earnestly pray to You about:

_____

_____

_____

_____

_____

Day 5

"Limo Please!"

There it sat in the horseshoe driveway of the church, sparkling in the sunlight. A stretch limousine awaited the bride and groom as we were leaving their wedding ceremony. Seven-year-old Naomi stopped in her tracks to marvel at the impressively extended vehicle.

"Wow Mommy! That limo sure is long and pretty," admired Naomi. "Do you think the driver would give me a ride in it before the bride and groom come out?" she asked.

"No honey," I responded, "it's only for the bride and groom because it's their special day. One day when you get married, you'll get to ride in a limo with your husband."

"What?" my daughter complained, "I have to wait until I get *married?* That's such a long time from now Mommy. I can't wait that long!"

"Well, you'll just have to wait and be patient," I insisted.

Naomi sighed and mumbled sadly, "I want to ride in the limo now. The only other time I'll get to ride in a limo is when I'm dead. And then I won't even know that I'm riding in it."

Amused at her confusion, I laughed and explained, "That kind of car is not a limousine Naomi. It's called a hearse."

"See!" Naomi exclaimed, "I won't even get to ride in a limo when I'm dead so that's another reason I should ride in this one right now!"

We say "no" or "wait" to our children for their own good. As parents, we have a long-term view of what's best for them. We see pitfalls they can't see. We see the downside to them getting what they are begging for in the moment and the benefit of waiting patiently to receive it later.

Even though we often compel our children to be patient, we don't like to hear that message from God. Waiting patiently for something we earnestly desire can be challenging to say the least. Practicing delayed gratification is a powerful discipline, but it usually doesn't feel good at the time. Like my daughter, sometimes we rationalize why getting what we desire at a later time just won't be as good as getting it now. Trusting God and His timing seems impossible in those moments. Yet those are the times we need to trust Him the most and be patient.

Oh that our children would have faith in our judgment as parents and wait patiently, whether it feels good to them or not. Likewise, we should trust God when He says *wait patiently, not just yet*, or *no for now*. Surely God sees what we can't see, and knows what we don't know. We can trust Him as we wait patiently for His perfect timing.

But let patience have its perfect work, that you may be perfect and complete, lacking nothing.　　JAMES 1:4 (NKJV)

"For My thoughts are not your thoughts, nor are your ways My ways," says the Lord.　　ISAIAH 55:8 (NKJV)

Think it Through: What is one area of your life in which you are currently struggling with patience?

Make it Personal: Lord, thank You for developing patience in my life by not giving me everything I want when I want it. Help me to fully trust that You know

what's best for me, and accept Your will. Today, help me
to be patient for:

_____

_____

_____

_____

_____

Day 6

❧

I'm a Big Girl

"Lord, thank You for giving me two big sisters to help me," six-year-old Joy often prayed at bedtime. In response to Joy's lovely sentiment, eight-year-old Naomi sarcastically noted one evening:

> I don't know why Joy always prays that. Every time we try to help her with something she says, "No, I don't need any help! I'm a big girl. I can do it by myself."

Perhaps Joy's day to day actions weren't quite matching the words of her nighttime prayer! At least in her big sister's eyes, there was a definite contradiction in what Joy was praying at night and what she was doing throughout the day.

So what about us grown-up girls? How often do we intellectually acknowledge that God is always here to help us, but then we go off and do things our own way? At times, we don't even seek God first in prayer before making key decisions—which is in essence saying, *"No, I don't need any help. I'm a big girl. I can do it by myself!"*

I confess. Big-girl syndrome strikes me more often than I'd like to admit, and I'm usually kicking myself afterward. I attempt to accomplish something in my own strength instead of asking God to fill me with His power. Then I wonder why I'm overwhelmed and burned out. It's so easy to become overly confident in our skills, talent, and intellect—which might carry us to a certain point of success. However, our lack of ability and power becomes painfully evident when we get to the end of ourselves. We realize we've been operating from a human power source that cannot go the distance to complete what God has called us to do.

The truth is God's wisdom and power are needed in every aspect of our lives, especially in raising our precious gifts from God. From the monotonous tasks of managing a household, to training and guiding our children, to modeling the character of Christ in our own lives—without God, there's no way we can make it.

We will never be perfect. God never calls us to perfection. But He does call us to seek Him with our hearts, souls, and minds. He desires for us to faithfully read and apply His Word that is full of wisdom and guidance. He delights in us depending on the power of the Holy Spirit to accomplish what we cannot do in our own strength and abilities.

Do you all too often find yourself being a "big girl"? Let's focus on being daughters of the Most High God, always in need of constant help from Abba Father.

I lift my eyes toward the mountains. Where will my help come from? My help comes from the Lord.

PSALM 121:1-2 (CSB)

Think it Through: In what area of your life are you trying to be a "big girl" and do things in your own power? Surrender that issue to God in prayer.

Make it Personal: Lord, I confess that sometimes I try to do things in my own power instead of relying on You for strength. I want to trust Your Holy Spirit to be my power source of strength. Today, I surrender:

_____

_____

_____

_____

_____

Day 7

⁓◦⁓

Real Dad

"Let's do another one!" squealed seven-year-old Naomi as we snuggled on her bed one evening. She carefully turned to the next page in the bright pink mother-daughter devotional, and I read the following instructions: *Mom, tell your daughter about a time you learned to trust God in a new way.* After a brief moment, I knew the exact story I wanted to share. Naomi inched closer to me and I began:

> *I will never forget when you were two years old, and you fell and hit your head on the edge of the fireplace. The blood was gushing out so fast I didn't think it would ever stop. I felt so helpless as Daddy strapped*

you into your car seat and drove you off to the emergency room. As soon as he backed out of the garage, I broke down into tears and started praying. That was the first time it really hit me that I couldn't protect you all of the time. I had to trust that God was protecting you, even when bad things were happening.

Tears welled in my eyes, and my voice cracked a little, but I managed to continue:

That night, I finally accepted that God is your real Father and Protector. He has just loaned you to me and Daddy to raise for His glory.

I gazed into my daughter's eyes at that emotional, spiritually-rich moment and waited for her response. She looked puzzled and questioned, "So-o-o-o-o-o *Daddy's* not my real father?" Suddenly, my touching spiritual moment wasn't feeling so touching anymore! Frustrated, I briskly stood up, switched off the bedroom light and sighed, "Goodnight Naomi." As I left her bedroom shaking my head in dismay she cried out, "So are you my real mother?"

Apparently my well-intended story resulted in more confusion than clarity. And for some of us, the idea of a father who unconditionally loves and protects his children can seem just as baffling and far-fetched. Traumatic and disheartening life experiences can leave us feeling abandoned. Mistreatment by those who should have loved and protected us can cause us to feel unworthy of God's love. Unwise choices can make us doubt if God would ever have anything to do with us. Yet nothing can keep the God of the universe from desiring to be our Heavenly Father.

God's Word lovingly explains that becoming His child involves a simple yet significant decision: placing our faith in what His Son Jesus did on the cross for us. Jesus was brutally crucified and died to pay the price for our sins. When we confess that we are sinners and invite Christ to come into our hearts, we accept this payment for our sins. It's a gift from God, and the sacrificial blood of Jesus cleanses us of our sin. As a result, we gain eternal life with God in Heaven after we leave this earth. God sacrificed His only Son so that we could spend eternity with Him. Does John 3:16 sound familiar?

For God so loved the world that he gave his one and only Son, that whoever believes in him shall not perish but have eternal life. (NIV)

Yes, accepting Christ into your heart as your personal Savior grants you eternal life. Receiving salvation also begins the journey of growing into the purpose God has for you as His creation. It all begins with believing that Jesus is the Son of God and placing your faith in what He freely did on the cross—just for you.

As a daughter of the King, I receive endless unconditional love. God loves and forgives me over and over again—no matter how many times I mess up. I don't have to prove myself to Him or try to impress Him. He walks with me through the struggles of life. As I trust Him more and more, He molds me into the person He has designed for me to become.

If you haven't already asked Jesus to come into your heart, there's no better time to do so than right now. Take this moment to make sure you are indeed a child of the Living God. You can say the prayer below, or express your heart to God in your own words. The Word of God is crystal clear; He is patiently and lovingly waiting to become your Father.

Yet to all who did receive him, to those who believed in his name, he gave the right to become children of God.

JOHN 1:12 (NIV)

Think it Through: Have you ever asked Jesus to come into your heart and forgive you for your sins? If not, what's keeping you from taking that step? Place your faith in Christ right now through a prayer from your heart.

Make it Personal: God, I want to be Your child. I want to give my life to You. Today, (date) _____ , I confess that I am a sinner in need of forgiveness. Thank You for sending Your Son Jesus to die on the cross for my sins. I put my faith in what Jesus did for me, and I accept Jesus into my heart to be my Savior and Lord. Thank You for giving me eternal life in Heaven with You. Now grow me into the person You want me to be. Amen.

_____

_____

_____

_____

_____

Day 8

"...99, 100!"

"Mommy, can I be in the talent show at the church?" asked four-year-old Lydia.

"I guess so," replied my sister reluctantly, "but what talent are you going to do?"

"I'm going to count to 100!" bragged my niece.

My sister wasn't quite sure how to break it to her daughter that counting to one hundred might not be considered a talent. She paused for a moment to think of an explanation that might encourage her daughter to reconsider.

"Lydia sweetheart," my sister began, "it's great that you can count to 100, but I think the showcase is for talents like singing, dancing, playing the piano—things like that."

"That's fine," Lydia acknowledged, "but I want to count to 100," insisted my niece. My sister ultimately conceded to her daughter's wishes.

The night of the talent show, my sister felt a bit apprehensive—understandably so. While other children would be performing "regular" talents, her daughter was going to count to one hundred. Soon it was my niece's turn, and she approached the microphone shyly with her mom by her side. Gripping my sister's pant leg, Lydia suddenly announced, "I'm going to count to 100!"

Carefully and deliberately, Lydia began: "One… two…three…four…". My sister clenched her teeth and thought, *I cannot believe this! My daughter is counting to 100 for a talent, and she has the nerve to do it slowly.*

". . . 55, 56, 57 . . ." Lydia steadily continued. The audience listened patiently, and after what seemed like an eternity to my sister, Lydia proudly declared: ". . . 98, 99, 100!"

To my sister's surprise, the crowd erupted into applause and cheered for Lydia as if she had won a gold medal in the Olympics! Who knew counting to one hundred could be so inspiring?

My mommy-heart was filled with encouragement after hearing this story. There are countless duties we carry out that may not seem very significant: picking up toys for the 57th time, packing school lunches, folding piles of laundry, helping with homework, and the list goes on and on. Completing such daily tasks can seem as unimpressive as counting to one hundred. But even if no one else appears to value all we do as moms, God is cheering us on from above. It is a high calling from God to be a mother and care for your home and the people in it. God thinks everything you do to make your house a home—one task at a time—is a big deal.

We may not get rousing applause from our children, husbands, or anyone else on any given day. However, we can know that God sees our endless efforts and sacrifices for our families, *and He is clapping like crazy!* So moms, keep counting to one hundred. Our Heavenly Father is indeed truly impressed.

Whatever you do, do it from the heart, as something done for the Lord and not for people.   Colossians 3:23 (csb)

Think it Through: Does knowing God values all you do as a mother encourage you? What voices cause you to feel insignificant in your role as a mom? Does one of those voices belong to you?

Make it Personal: Lord, thank You for placing a high value on all I do as a mom. When I am discouraged or looking for the approval of others, help me find comfort in knowing that You see my role as significant. I will encourage another mom today by:

_____

_____

_____

_____

_____

Day 9

Minivan Moment

I wonder how many hours I've racked up driving my kids around in our minivan? Or maybe I really *don't* want to know. After our third munchkin came along, seldom did I have only one daughter in tow as we traveled about from day to day. On those rare occasions, I'd sometimes ask that lone little lady to share anything she might have on her mind. It might be a question or problem, or perhaps something personal she wanted to talk to mommy about without her siblings being within earshot.

I'd generally start by asking: "So, is there anything on your mind you want to talk about since it's just you and me?" Most times, a question, request, or recent adventure became the topic of discussion.

One minivan ride with six-year-old Naomi was truly a memorable moment. Before I could ask her my standard opening question, she sweetly inquired, "So Mommy, is there anything on your mind that *you* want to talk about?" Pleasantly surprised by her question, I stumbled with my response, "Well, nothing I can think of right now." She had caught me off guard! "By the way," I continued, "what made you ask me that?" Naomi graciously replied, "You always ask that question when it's just you and me. So this time, I thought I'd ask you first!"

I wonder how God would feel if we took the time to ask Him for *His* thoughts first before we pray? To be honest, I'm usually guilty of immediately pouring out my heart, my wishes, my needs, and my wants when I talk to God. But what if from time to time I approached Him with a prayer-posture that conveys, *"Father, I just want to hear from You first."*

It's challenging to resist the urge to instantly rattle off the I-Need-God-To-Do lists we have each day. However, the rewards could be immeasurable with the alternate approach of pausing to listen for His voice first. You just might hear answers you have long been awaiting, or a sweet whisper from the Father that affirms His love and comfort towards you. You might gain direction on how to bless or encourage someone, or feel an urgency to pray for a family member or friend. Perhaps God will instruct you to take specific steps to heal a relationship. Maybe you'll hear a gentle but necessary rebuke that leads to restoration.

Whatever the Lord conveys, as you intentionally listen for His Voice, your prayer time with Him will surely be worthwhile moments to treasure.

The Lord came and stood there, calling as at the other times, "Samuel! Samuel!" Then Samuel said, "Speak, for your servant is listening." 1 SAMUEL 3:10 (NIV)

Think it Through: Insert your name in the following Scripture: The Lord came and stood there, calling as at the other times, " _____ ,

_____ !" Now say, "Speak Lord, for your servant is listening." What do you hear God impressing upon your heart?

Make it Personal: Lord, help me to be more mindful of asking You to speak to me and pausing to listen for Your voice. Incline my ears to be sensitive and obedient to all You have to say to me.

_____

_____

_____

_____

_____

Day 10

Fish-Killer

It all started with the October daddy-and-his-daughters date. My husband Jeff proudly escorted our three girls to the annual church harvest festival. One year, each daughter won a goldfish—the prize for successfully tossing a ping-pong ball into a tiny bowl containing the bright-orange creature with bulging eyes. On the way home from the festival, the girls insisted on stopping to purchase fish food for their new pets.

Joy and Naomi, ages seven and nine at the time, couldn't resist shaking the colorful flakes of food into the fish bowls. Jeff warned that the fish could die from over-feeding, but the girls continued to sprinkle away.

Eventually, my husband moved the fish food to a cabinet shelf the girls couldn't reach. He admonished them to feed the fish only once a day.

Unfortunately, by the next morning, one of our three fish friends had gone belly up. By day two, Joy's fish was resting (or shall I say floating) in peace. Joy cried and mourned over the loss of her precious fish Goldie. To make matters worse, Naomi began declaring that their *dad* had killed the fish by limiting the feedings to only once a day.

In hopes of quieting the accusations of fish-starvation, I grabbed the fish food bottle from the shelf so Naomi could feed the lone survivor. Reading the back of the bottle, Naomi exclaimed, "Daddy was wrong! It says right here to feed the fish *three* times a day!" In disbelief, I snatched the bottle from her hand and squinted to read the microscopic print on the back. Sure enough, Naomi was correct. Three times a day.

As allegations of my husband being a fish-killer continued to abound, I tried to turn the tide in a different direction. Attempting to calm the girls down and perhaps instill a sense of gratitude, I quickly noted, "Hey, if it wasn't for Daddy taking you to the harvest festival, you all never would have even gotten the fish." Naomi frowned and snapped back, "Yeah, but if it wasn't for Daddy, we'd *still* have the fish."

When things don't go as we expect or desire, it's tempting to blame others. We can't see past our anger, anxiety, or grief in that moment of disappointment. And when no human is readily available to blame, God can become a convenient target.

Disappointment also has a way of giving us short memories. We tend to focus on the current predicament and see only the proverbial half-empty glass. We forget God is still in control and has a plan. We forget all the times He made a way in the past; all the times He protected and provided for us; all the times He loved us when we were unlovable.

During difficult times is exactly when we need to focus most on the goodness and sovereignty of God. If He is allowing a trial in your life, there's a purpose for it. There's something for you to gain. Romans 8:28 assures us that God works all things together for our good according to His purposes—even the hardships of life.

The next time you're tempted to doubt God in the midst of a trial, press pause and take a breath. God always has your best interest at heart, no matter the situation. Whatever you are going through, His love for you is eternal.

We know that all things work together for the good of those who love God, who are called according to his purpose.

ROMANS 8:28 (CSB)

Look, I am the Lord, the God over every creature. Is anything too difficult for me? JEREMIAH 32:27 (CSB)

Think it Through: Think of a time you were angry with God or blamed Him because a situation did not turn out the way you desired: _____

_____

Can you see how God has brought some good to you or others through that very situation? If you can't, ask God to help you trust that He indeed has a purpose for that trial in your life.

Make it Personal: Lord, I confess the times I have been angry with You. Thank You for Your forgiveness. Help me remember that You always know what's best for me, even when I don't understand why certain hardships happen. Help me to remember how You have always been there for me, and that You will never leave me.

_____

_____

_____

_____

Day 11

Tooth Fairy Tales

*A*pparently I wasn't very good at pretending there was such a thing as the Tooth Fairy. In my defense, it wasn't due to a lack of effort on my part. I got a major mommy-thrill from the whole charade, but for some reason, my kids just weren't buying it.

"Mommy, *you* are the Tooth Fairy!" they each accused. Nevertheless, I continued to claim I only delivered their baby teeth to a magical fairy, who in turn left coins or little trinkets under their pillows. Since I remained committed to my little game, my kids indulged me and played along.

During a meal at a family restaurant, nine-year-old Naomi skillfully plucked a loose tooth from her mouth with her tiny fingers. In comparison to the other teeth she had lost in the past, this tooth was farther back in her mouth and was "big" in her eyes. Proud of her accomplishment, Naomi left the following note for the Tooth Fairy that evening:

Dear TF,

I would like $2.00 for my tooth tonight. Thanks!

XOXO,

Naomi

Chart
$1.00 = regular tooth
$1.50 = tooth came out at a special time or place
$2.00 = back tooth plus all of the above

P.S. U should copy this chart.

Playing the Tooth Fairy game can be harmless enough. But treating God like He is some sort of magical fairy is an entirely different story. We somehow have the notion that God should compensate us accordingly for our noble efforts, or that we can earn extra points with Him. Even if it's subconscious, we tend to expect some form of reward in our lives for "good behavior."

On the flip side, if we experience a seemingly undeserved hardship, we might find ourselves thinking something along the lines of: *Why is this happening to me? I'm a good person. I go to church, read my Bible, donate to charities, and help out my co-workers. I'm nice to my neighbors. I don't deserve this.* The underlying mindset is the notion that God owes us for "living right."

Of course, the Father is pleased when we honor Him with our lives and serve others in love. But those things don't obligate Him to bless us like a spiritual formula. The truth is we really don't deserve and can never earn any of God's blessings. No matter what we do or don't do, He graciously chooses to bless us simply because He is a loving God.

For starters, God graces us with the eternal gift of salvation (Ephesians 2:8-10). He provides for our earthly needs. He walks with us through our trials and challenges. He comforts us in our grief. He accepts us as we are. He forgives us when we confess our sins. He gives us the ability to love others as He loves us. He does exceedingly and abundantly more than we can ever ask or think (Ephesians 3:20)! He goes far beyond what any of us deserves.

God blesses us not because we are good, but because He is so good. He only calls us to diligently seek Him (Hebrews 11:6). It's a relief to know we don't have to negotiate with God for rewards or blessings based on our deeds. Instead, we can serve Him from a pure heart to bring glory to His name and kingdom. We can expect great things from God, but not because we've earned them or deserve them. He lovingly gives it all by His grace.

God's grace has saved you because of your faith in Christ. Your salvation doesn't come from anything you do. It is God's gift. It is not based on anything you have done. No one can brag about earning it. Ephesians 2:8-9 (NIrV)

Think it Through: Do you feel you have to earn God's blessings by being a good person? Do you sometimes think you deserve or are owed rewards in your life for being obedient, serving others, or doing good works? Are you sometimes motivated to do a good deed to gain favor with God?

Make it Personal: Lord, help me to remember that I don't have to bargain with You, nor can I earn Your favor or blessings. Let me serve You purely out of a heart that loves and trusts You, without expectation of an earthly reward. I confess the times I've felt I was 'owed' the blessings of:

_____

_____

_____

_____

_____

Day 12

Doughnuts

Three-year-old Jameson loved spending time with his Uncle Dan. One particular afternoon, Jameson was looking forward to one of their favorite uncle-and-nephew outings: a trip to the nearby doughnut shop. As usual, they made their trek to the bakery, carefully chose their treats, and headed back to the house to enjoy the sugar rush.

After getting situated at the kitchen table, Uncle Dan grinned at his nephew and declared, "Thank you Jesus for this food." Jameson stared quizzically at his uncle and replied, "But Uncle Dan, I'm not Jesus. I'm Jameson!"

Jameson is spot on. We too should be intentional about acknowledging God as the one who provides for us. After all, one of His Old Testament names is Jehovah-Jireh, the God who provides.

The journey of learning to trust God as our ultimate provider can feel like riding a see-saw. On one end, there are times we worry if or how God is going to provide in a distressing circumstance—perhaps an unexpected medical bill, a totaled vehicle, or a random job loss. On the other end, there are times we foolishly place confidence in our own abilities, independent of God. We put trust in our vocations and careers, educational degrees, skills, talents, and bank accounts. We can even become prideful in the false security of self-sufficiency.

It can be dizzying to see-saw back and forth between worry and foolish pride. The sweet-spot is balancing right in the middle. The Bible instructs us to cast our cares on God whenever we start to worry (1 Peter 5:7). Simultaneously, we must remain humble during the times provision and blessings are flowing in our lives. We must not forget to give God the glory for all we have.

By trusting God as the Source of all our resources, we can rest in knowing He will surely take care of every need. Fully acknowledge that God deserves the credit and praise for everything He provides for you. After all, your name isn't Jesus either.

Instruct those who are rich in the present age not to be arrogant or to set their hope on the uncertainty of wealth, but on God, who richly provides us with all things to enjoy.

1 TIMOTHY 6:17 (CSB)

Every good and perfect gift is from above, coming down from the Father of lights. JAMES 1:17A (CSB)

Therefore I tell you, do not worry about your life . . . Can any one of you by worrying add a single hour to your life? MATTHEW 6:25-27 (NIV)

Think it Through: Today, make a point to notice every single thing God provides for you and your family, and thank Him. If you've been taking credit for any blessings in your life, confess and commit to adopting a new mindset of acknowledging God as the one who provides.

Make it Personal: Lord, help me to always recognize you as Jehovah-Jireh, the one who provides. Whenever I am tempted to worry or boast in myself, in money, or anything else as my source, remind me that You are my Provider. Today, I praise Your name especially for:

_____

_____

_____

_____

_____

_____

_____

_____

Day 13

Figs and Wigs

Wearing a wig is something I never anticipated I'd do. Nothing against wigs, they're just out of my hairstyle comfort zone. Unfortunately, a gradually expanding bald spot on the crown of my head left me little choice but to temporarily wear a wig for a few months. I felt self-conscious because the wig didn't look as natural as I had hoped. But I finally gathered enough courage to reveal my new hairdo for the first time at a morning church service.

My church convenes several services each Sunday with literally thousands of people attending throughout the day. I was confident I could hide in the crowd to some degree. However, I knew eventually I'd see people who would surely know the wig was not my real hair.

As I greeted various friends and acquaintances, to my surprise and relief, no one said a thing about my wig. Perhaps they were just being nice and didn't want to make an awkward scene, and that was fine with me. By the time our pastor had completed his sermon, I had pretty much forgotten about my flowing fake hair.

At the end of the church service, my husband and I exited the sanctuary and headed towards the Sunday school wing to pick up our kids. Seven-year-old Naomi bounced from her classroom to greet me among a sea of people in the busy hallway. Sounding like an intercom announcement, she suddenly exclaimed, "Mommy, could anyone tell you're wearing a wig?" Freezing in my tracks, I knelt close to my daughter's ear and whispered in dismay, "Well if they couldn't tell *before*, I guess they can tell *now*." Then I gave her the mommy-evil-eye look! Can we say the word *embarrassed*?

At that moment, I could relate to Adam and Eve in the Garden of Eden. Instead of a wig, they were trying to hide behind fig leaves—knowing they were naked. I guess they were just hoping God wouldn't notice. Yet eventually, their sin of eating fruit from the one forbidden tree came to full light.

We've all tried in some way to cover flaws, mistakes, or outright sinful behavior. Though we may succeed at "fooling some of the people some of the time," we never fool God. Instead of trying to devise a cover-up, God's Word encourages us to be quick to confess our sins to Him and others (1 John 1:9, James 5:16).

There's no need to try to conceal anything from our God who loves us unconditionally and is willing to forgive all things we confess. Though it can be challenging, embarrassing, or outright humiliating at the time, choosing honesty before God and others is always a wise decision. Take it from me, fig leaves, a wig, or any other covering just never seems to work out in the long run.

If we confess our sins, he is faithful and just and will forgive us our sins and purify us from all unrighteousness.

1 JOHN 1:9 (NIV)

Therefore confess your sins to each other and pray for each other so that you may be healed. JAMES 5:16A (NIV)

Think it Through: When is the last time you tried to cover a flaw, mistake, or sin? Do you think you were successful? Did you confess your "covering" to God and ask forgiveness from anyone else who may have been involved?

Make it Personal: Lord, help me to always be honest before You and others. Whenever I am tempted to try to cover my sins, flaws, or innocent mistakes, remind me of Your great grace and forgiveness. Today I confess:

_____

_____

_____

_____

_____

Day 14

Are You Listening?

Clean bathrooms. Check. Reschedule dental appointment. Check. Reply to party Evite. Check.

I was determined to tame my never-ending To-Do list while eating lunch one Saturday afternoon. As usual, completing the next daily task was at the forefront of my mind. Seven-year-old Joy plopped down beside me at the dining table. She began excitedly telling me about a classroom event that happened at school earlier in the week. As I gobbled a bite and checked off another item on my list, I nodded my head towards Joy, mumbled a few "um-hums," and gave a little chuckle. Soon nine-year-old Naomi gently advised her sister:

Joy, you should just stop talking. Mommy's not really paying attention to you. That's just the laugh and noises she makes when she's trying to make you think she's listening, but really she's not.

Bust-ed! I guess I should have seen that coming. Had I chuckled about something Joy said that wasn't funny? Or was it just that obvious I wasn't in tune with my daughter as she was attempting to communicate with me? Probably both.

I shared this embarrassing moment with twelve-year-old Karis. Her response convicted me: "Wow Mom. I wonder if that's how God feels when He's trying to speak to us, but we're not really listening to Him." Ouch! Guilty as charged. Like when I rush through a devotion just to "get it in" for the day, or say a quick prayer without any real thought or taking the time to wait for God to speak. And please don't tell my pastor, but I've caught myself planning what needs to be done *after* church *during* the Sunday sermon! Can I get a witness?

It's counter-intuitive but sometimes the more we incorporate a spiritual discipline into our lives, the easier it becomes to rush through it, take it for granted, or multi-task through it. We have to jolt ourselves back into an intentional focus of hearing from God. Busyness can certainly be a distraction, and we all have a billion things on our plates any given day. But if we're too busy to listen to God, then we're just too busy.

Since the Maker of the universe is our Father, we might want to actually pay attention when He's trying to speak to our hearts. After all, He always knows if we are really listening.

My sheep listen to my voice; I know them, and they follow me.   JOHN 10:27 (NLT)

Think it Through: What on your agenda right now is making you "too busy" to hear from God? Take time today to just sit, meditate on a Bible passage, and listen for God to speak to your heart.

Make it Personal: Lord, forgive me for the times I have been distracted when You were trying to speak to me. Help me to slow down, focus on You, and listen for Your voice every day. At this moment, please speak to my heart. *(Write what you hear.)*

_____

_____

_____

_____

Day 15

❧

And Why are You Here?

We want our kids to tell the truth, right? Take eight-year-old Christopher, who didn't really want to be in the children's choir at church. However, his mom decided it would be a good experience to help him come out of his shell a bit more. She faithfully transported him to and from the Saturday morning choir rehearsals, hoping he'd eventually take an interest in singing and enjoy making friends in the group.

The children's choir performed beautifully one Sunday morning, with each little singer dressed neatly in crisp white and navy blue. At the end of the church service, the choir director approached Christopher's mom and reported with a smile:

> *I have to tell you about your son. At the beginning of yesterday's rehearsal, I asked the children, "So why are we here today?" I started going around the circle for answers. One child said, "I'm here to sing about God." Another child said, "I'm here to praise Jesus!" When it was Christopher's turn he answered, "I'm here because my mother made me come."*

Now that's honesty!

So let's get honest with ourselves. Do you ever find yourself wondering why you are here on this earth? Do you have a sense of purpose? Or are you trudging through, day to day, unsure about what you are supposed to accomplish with your life?

There's good news: God tells us our purpose. We have the distinct honor of being here on this earth as His workmanship (Ephesians 2:10). We are not here by random chance. God's Word declares He has fearfully and wonderfully created each of us (Psalm 139:13-14). We are ultimately here to bring Him glory with our lives. God gives each of us free will to make life choices that honor Him, or we can choose to live according to our own plans and standards.

God indeed has a tailored plan for your life. He sacrificed His only Son so that you might live life to the fullest (John 10:10). His plan is not for you to wander through life aimlessly, but instead to go with Him on a challenging yet purpose-filled journey. The map we have on that journey is God's Word, and our compass is Jesus Christ.

Have you started your journey with Christ? If not, begin today by committing your life to the Savior. Ask Jesus to come into your heart, forgive you of your sins, and grow you into the person He wants to you be.

If you have already begun this incredible journey with Jesus, dig into God's Word each day to continuously discover His will for your life. Spend time with God in prayer, seeking the purposes He has for you. Take time to listen to God and obey Him. Day by day, you can discover His plan for your life, which is indeed *why* you are really here.

For we are God's handiwork, created in Christ Jesus to do good works, which God prepared in advance for us to do.   EPHESIANS 2:10 (NIV)

For it was you who created my inward parts; you knit me together in my mother's womb. I will praise you because I have been remarkably and wondrously made.

PSALM 139:13-14A (CBS)

I have come in order that you might have life—
life in all its fullness. John 10:10b (GNT)

Think it Through: Do you live like you are here for a purpose? Or are you simply going through the motions, day by day? Being a mom gives you a unique purpose in life. God gave you the exact children He intended for you to have. How do you see your role as a mom giving God glory?

Make it Personal: Lord, I want to live my life with meaning and purpose for You. Help me to live in a way that brings You glory. Today as a mom, I can bring You glory by:

_____

_____

_____

_____

_____

Day 16

Cruise Control

With buttons to push, a big wheel to turn, and colorful blinking lights, seven-year-old Naomi was fascinated by the dashboard of our minivan. "10, 20, 30 . . . What do those numbers mean Mommy?" she inquired.

"That's the speedometer," I explained. "Those numbers tell you how fast you're driving. And it's time for us to get going."

"Can I finish counting?" Naomi pleaded with her *can-I-pleeeease* eyes. I reluctantly granted her request, and she continued.

". . . 100, 110, 120, 130!" Naomi proudly announced and bounced into her booster seat.

Once we got on the road, I pointed out a few speed limit signs and explained how patrol officers can give tickets to people who are driving over the speed limit.

"Mommy, what's the biggest number on a speed limit sign?" Naomi inquired.

"Oh, I've seen up to 70 miles per hour," I replied.

Naomi seemed satisfied with my response for a moment, but then reasoned, "Well then why do they even make cars that can go faster than 70 miles an hour? They should just make it so a car can't go over the speed limit. That way, no one would ever get a ticket!"

Perhaps car manufacturers will implement Naomi's idea someday. Until then, the next best thing drivers have to help ensure they stay within the boundary of the speed limit is the trusty cruise control feature. For drivers who find cruise control convenient, it's a helpful tool to make long road trips easier.

What if we could place our *lives* on cruise control? A *spiritual* cruise control. Our lives would be so much easier if we had a fool-proof way to stay within the protective boundaries God sets for us. What if we only had to press a few buttons to automatically live within the guidelines of God's Word?

Unfortunately, our journeys with Christ don't quite work that way. Just as speed limit signs only make us aware of a traffic safety boundary, God's Word only reveals His precepts designed to lovingly protect us. It's up to us to choose if we will accept His protection or not.

When we willfully decide to step outside of God's boundaries, it only results in harm or consequences to ourselves or others. God in His infinite wisdom has everyone's best interest at heart. Just as it's our choice to drive within the speed limit to help protect ourselves and others, it's our choice to stay within the boundaries God sets forth in His Word.

The Father also offers protective wisdom through His Word to help make us aware of His will for our lives. Again, it's our choice to either follow that wisdom, or we can foolishly operate within our own standards and reasoning instead.

Proverbs 3:5-6 advises:

> *Trust in the Lord with all your heart.*
> *Do not depend on your own understanding.*
> *In all your ways obey him.*
> *Then he will make your paths smooth and straight.* (NIrV)

Here's the truth: we have something much better than cruise control to aid us in decision-making as we follow Jesus. God has given us the gift of the Holy Spirit, and we can choose to rely on God's power moment by moment, day by day. Ephesians 5:18 implores us to be fully directed and influenced by the Spirit of God. If we truly desire, the Holy Spirit can be our inner GPS system.

Furthermore, the Bible is a priceless roadmap that when read, studied, and followed can lead us on God's intended path for our lives. But following our own wisdom will cause us to get off course, reach dead ends and roadblocks, and hit huge potholes we could have avoided. Yet even if we get off track, we can still choose to "re-route" and follow God's Word to be steered in the right direction.

Though the journey is by no means promised to be easy, you can pursue and fulfill the plans and purposes God has for your life. And that, my friend, is a road trip worth taking.

May Your gracious Spirit lead me on level ground.

PSALM 143:10B (CSB)

Your word is like a lamp that shows me the way. It is like a light that guides me. PSALM 119:105 (NIRV)

Think it Through: What area of your spiritual life do you wish you could place on "cruise control?" Take a moment to pray and ask God for one step you can make in His power to begin submitting this area of your life fully to Him.

Make it Personal: Lord, You already know that I struggle with _____ . Guide me through Your Word to the steps I must take to surrender this area of my life to You. The first step I can take based on Your Word is:

_____

_____

_____

_____

_____

Day 17

Thou Shall Not Add On

"Don't lie!" shouted five-year-old Joy. "Don't steal!" declared seven-year-old Naomi.

I was quite impressed with my kids' review of their Sunday school lesson about the Ten Commandments. "That's pretty good ladies," I commended. "Do you remember any others?"

The girls contemplated my question for a moment, then one of them announced, "Don't smoke!" Before I could make a correction, the other child (apparently remembering a sign we'd seen at the playground) blurted out, "Don't litter!" I had to stop them from adding on more "commandments" before God's ten became thirteen or fourteen! Apparently, my children felt a couple of other guiding principles were worthy of being considered right up there with the top ten God gave the children of Israel.

Unfortunately, as moms, we have our own commandment-like standards that we apply to our children. One might think some of the expectations we have are truly biblical commands based on how we respond if they are "broken":

- *"Thou shall never be too noisy."*
- *"Thou shall never drop, spill, nor break anything."*
- *"Thou shall never embarrass me in public."*

Of course there's the go-to command we readily use: *"Thou shall always remember to* _____ *."* Insert: *brush your teeth . . . lock the front door . . . take your medicine . . . clean your room*—whatever the child has neglected to do for the 1039th time!

Yes, our children need to learn how to be responsible. And yes, parenting can be the most frustrating job *ever* at times. However, when our children don't meet our expectations, it is not breaking a Commandment. And we shouldn't react as if it is.

We all lose it from time to time. This parenting journey entails countless occasions of discouragement, disappointment, and disillusionment with our children and ourselves. When that happens, we can intentionally take a moment to breathe, calm down, and then extend grace. Granting grace to our children is definitely a more productive response than spouting off made-up commandments. We can learn to express our frustration in ways that not only provide direction but are also seasoned with grace.

A little grace can go a long way when it comes to parenting. It certainly doesn't hurt for us to remember that even as God's grown-up children, we never have and never will master commandment-keeping. We are human and fallible, just like our kids. What a precious opportunity we have as parents to model extending grace, the very grace God so freely grants to us.

The Lord is gracious and full of compassion, slow to anger and great in mercy. PSALM 145:8 (NKJV)

Think it Through: What are some of your "commandments" for your children? Are they reasonable expectations? How can you temper your reaction to include grace when your expectations aren't met by your children?

Make it Personal: Lord, I confess sometimes I hold my children to unreasonable standards and expectations. Help me extend grace to them and not overreact in anger or dismay. Let me remember the grace and new mercies You extend to me each day. One expectation of my children I need to temper with grace is:

_____

_____

_____

_____

_____

Day 18

※

Lemons

"That's the way the cookie crumbles," I remarked to my daughters one day. Nine-year-old Naomi asked the meaning of this cookie-phrase, which led to a conversation about idioms (I call them "sayings") and the truths you can find in them. I gave my daughter a few more examples: *don't bite off more than you can chew; kill two birds with one stone; you can't judge a book by its cover . . .* soon she got the point.

A few days later, we were watching a television show and a character exclaimed, "When life gives you lemons, make lemonade!"

"Mom, is that one of those sayings you were talking about?" Naomi inquired.

"Yes!" I replied. "That's a good one."

"Well, unless you have some water and a whole bunch of sugar," Naomi continued, "that sure is gonna be some sour lemonade." Touché!

I don't know about you, but when I feel surrounded by nothing but lemons, I can't even begin to imagine how to possibly make lemonade. I feel especially discouraged when I'm trying my best to follow God, yet find myself in a place of confusion and discouragement. I start focusing on what I believe the missing ingredients are in my situation and fretting over what I don't have. I convince myself: *surely nothing good is going to come from this!* Disheartened, I'm tempted to abandon the goal, discontinue the course, or quit the race.

Life can seem like a 1,000-piece puzzle. We can't see the beauty of the finished product because all the pieces aren't in place yet. We must remember God created the exact design of the puzzle with a specific purpose in mind, and He has all the pieces. He knows exactly when and where they are to go in place. He has already seen the wondrously complete picture that will be created in the end if we don't quit.

In the book of Psalms, David describes the Word of God as a lamp to his feet and a light to his path (Psalm 119:105). God gives us just enough light to see right where we are standing, and maybe a few steps further down the path. Particularly when we're in a "lemon" situation, we'd prefer to have a gigantic floodlight to see the entire terrain in front of us. The current lamp at our feet allows us to only view the immediate roadblock, and we feel there is no way to move ahead. Yet if we don't take that next step, we will never reach the final destination God has in mind.

It's natural to feel discouraged when all you seem to have is lemons. But keep pressing forward on the path God has for you. Place your faith and trust in Him—unlimited resources are at His disposal. Maintain hope that in the right timing, He'll eventually provide all the water and sugar you need to make sweet, refreshing lemonade with those lemons.

And my God will supply all your needs according to his riches in glory in Christ Jesus. PHILIPPIANS 4:19 (CSB)

Think it Through: When has God provided a need in your life in an unexpected manner or at an unexpected time? What need do you currently have? Will you trust God to provide it in His time and in His way? Choose a Scripture to focus on while you trust God to provide your need.

Make it Personal: Lord, because You have provided for me time after time, I can trust You to provide my current needs. Help me to be patient as I wait for Your provision. Show me if there is anything You are waiting for me to do first, and give me a mind of obedience to do it. Today I trust You to provide:

_____

_____

_____

_____

_____

Day 19

A $1 Sacrifice

"Are we really gonna see the *President's* desk at the White House?" Naomi asked in awe. Through a colleague, my husband had arranged a family tour of the West Wing—including the Oval Office. On the day of our tour, we were excited and a bit nervous as we made our way through the security checkpoints, not knowing what to expect. Sure enough, something unexpected was about to happen to me as a mother that I will never forget.

At the halfway point of the tour, our White House guide offered us a quick break at a small bathroom. I allowed my girls to go first and instructed them to wait for me at the end of the hallway. As I exited the restroom,

to my utter dismay I see my 8 and 10-year-olds prac-
tically fighting over who would sit in the lone hallway
chair! As only kids can, they were pushing and shoving
trying to squeeze two bottoms into a chair that could
obviously fit only one person. As I hurried down the
hallway fuming, I noticed my 12-year-old casually opening and closing the drawer of a wooden side table, as well
as clicking the table's decorative lamp off and on . . . over
and over. *That pushed me over the edge.* All I could think
was, "Did I really have to tell you not to touch anything
in the *White House?*"

We completed the remainder of our tour without
further incident. Still, once we returned to our minivan, I wanted to make it crystal clear to my kids how
disappointed I was with their antics in the hallway. On
the drive home, they got the seriously extended version
of that mama speech about at least *acting* like they have
home-training in public!

Later that night, my husband found a slip of paper on
one of our bedroom pillows. It was a sweet note of apology from our 10-year-old. To our amazement, carefully
wrapped inside the note was a crumpled one-dollar bill.

You would have to know how much *this* particular
child adores money to know how astounding it is that
she included cash with her apology. *This* child negoti-
ates, bargains, and constantly tries to obtain money any

way she can. We knew she must have truly been sorry because she sacrificed something valuable to her to try to make amends. I must admit, it worked.

My daughter's gesture made me think: *what am I willing to sacrifice to show God how much I value my relationship with Him?* Am I willing to give up watching late-night movies to wake up earlier and spend more time in His Word? Am I willing to fast and pray for a circumstance God has placed on my heart (Matthew 6:17-18)? Am I willing to take time to help a friend, a neighbor, or a stranger—even if I'm incredibly "busy" at the moment? Am I willing to hold my tongue when I'm angry, instead of expressing every emotional thought that races through my head?

The choices we make do indeed reflect how much we value our relationship with our heavenly Father. Unfortunately, sometimes our actions, words, and priorities don't match what we say we value most.

Certainly one indication of how much we value someone or something is what we are willing to sacrifice. How great our Father's love must be for us! He sacrificed His only Son (John 3:16). Though we can never match this ultimate display of love, we can determine what needs to be sacrificed in our own lives to grow closer to God. If God is truly our highest priority, we should be willing to sacrifice anything and every-thing to draw closer to Him.

For God loved the world in this way: He gave his one and only Son. JOHN 3:16A (CSB)

"If anyone wants to be My follower, he must deny himself, take up his cross, and follow Me." MARK 8:34B (CSB)

Think it Through: What might God be calling you to sacrifice to gain a more intimate relationship with Him? What in your life seems "harmless" but is really a distraction to spending more time with God or grow-ing in your walk with Him? Television? Movies? Social Media? Food? Money? Busyness?

Make it Personal: Lord, show me the distractions in my life that are keeping me from getting closer to You. Help me be willing to sacrifice those things to make my relationship with You the number one priority in my life. One thing I can sacrifice this week is:

_____

_____

_____

_____

_____

Day 20

❧

All About Accessories

"Wake up ladies! A rest stop is coming up," my husband announced from the driver's seat. Our family was halfway through a ten-hour road trip. My daughters and I stretched and sluggishly put on our shoes as we prepared to exit our minivan. Through the sun visor mirror, I noticed ten-year-old Naomi in the captain seat behind me putting on lip gloss. She proceeded to put on earrings, fix her hair, and straighten her clothes. I took a quick look at myself in the mirror. My hair was a mess, and I certainly did not have on make-up or earrings. "Honey, we're just at a rest stop," I chuckled. "You don't need to put on lip gloss and earrings." Naomi shifted her eyes towards me and explained, "Well, this *is* just a rest stop, but I don't want to *look like* I've been traveling." Though she ended her statement there, her face was saying, *"But I can see you obviously don't care about looking a hot mess in public!"*

I had to admit I looked disheveled to say the least. It was true, I didn't care about my appearance because it was *just a rest stop.* However, once inside the bathroom, I saw my reflection in a full-length mirror. I indeed looked much worse than I thought! *"I guess Naomi has a point,"* I mumbled to myself. *"I could have at least tried to fix my hair."*

Once I made my way back to the minivan, it was my turn at the wheel. I climbed into the driver's seat and decided to put my hair in a clip to keep it out of my face. While I was looking in the rearview mirror to adjust the hair clip, Naomi returned to the minivan and taunted, "Oh *noooow* you try to fix your hair!"

I shared that story with my friend Jualecia who has an equally appearance-conscious, fashion-minded daughter. We laughed at the great lengths our daughters go through to ensure that with each outfit they wear, every accessory and piece of clothing is perfectly coordinated and in place. My friend made a powerful comment: "Our daughters put more effort into dressing and accessorizing each day than most of us put into preparing spiritually for the day. What if we were that deliberate about putting on our *spiritual armor* every day?"

Wow. My wise friend was referring to the pieces of spiritual armor described in the book of Ephesians. This armor provides protection and includes one vital weapon we must use to fight against the enemy. Yes, the enemy and his spiritual forces constantly try to derail, discourage, and defeat us at every turn. However, God gives us invaluable armor to protect us, as well as a weapon to fight with in this spiritual battle.

The pieces of armor are (Ephesians 6:14-17):
- *the belt of truth*
- *the breastplate of righteousness*
- *shoes ready with the gospel of peace*
- *the shield of faith*
- *the helmet of salvation*
- *the sword of the Spirit (God's Word)*

I certainly need every piece of that battle gear from day to day, and I'm willing to bet you do as well.

My daughter was simply going to a rest stop bathroom, and she took the time to make sure everything she was wearing was in place. We go into battle every day against the enemy of our souls, and some days, we barely take time to strap on any of the armor God gives us to be victorious. Let's be more intentional about fully covering ourselves with the armor of God so we can stand strong in the fight against the enemy and his kingdom of evil and darkness . . . "and having done all, to stand" (Ephesians 6:13b - NIV).

Put on the full armor of God so that you can stand against the schemes of the devil. For our struggle is not against flesh and blood, but against the rulers, against the authorities, against the cosmic powers of this darkness, against evil, spiritual forces in the heavens.

EPHESIANS 6:11-12 (CSB)

Think it Through: Do you take time to strap on your spiritual armor each morning? Or do you leave yourself easily open to the attacks of the enemy? What can you do to remind yourself each day for a month to put on your spiritual armor? Place a note on your mirror or dashboard, or put an index card in your Bible or journal. Ask your children for ideas and make it a family affair!

Make it Personal: Lord, help me to be more conscious about using the protection and weapons of warfare You have provided to help me fight the enemy. Today, I make a deliberate effort to focus on this piece of my spiritual armor: _____ , so that I can fight against:

_____

_____

_____

_____

Day 21

Never Outdated

$\mathcal{I}$ guess it happens to every mom . . . that day you realize your children think you're old—really old. I'll never forget one of my kids asking if TV had been invented by the time I was born. TV? *Really*? What was I, a relic?

I didn't help my case by attempting to explain what a pager was to 11-year-old Karis. Explaining how pagers were the big thing prior to cell phones, I shared how doctors, attorneys, and other professionals used the device, as well as people in everyday life.

My daughter asked, "So could you text a message to the pager?"

"Well, not exactly," I explained. "You could send a telephone number to a pager, or number messages like '911' to express an emergency."

"Could you call back the number you got on the pager?" Karis inquired.

"Yes!" I replied. "You just had to find the closest phone."

"What?" she responded with dismay. "You couldn't call the person back from the pager?"

"No, not from the actual pager," I admitted.

"Wow," my daughter concluded, "I can see why this device didn't last very long. It was basically useless!"

No matter how much I tried to convince my daughter of the value of a pager, she wasn't buying it. Compared to the modern-day cell phone, a pager didn't stand a chance in her eyes. And there are certainly other technological devices that at one point in time seem invaluable, yet are eventually considered outdated or of little use.

But there's a book that's been around for hundreds of years, and it still holds priceless value. It proves to be indispensable for anyone who dares to believe the words contained inside. That book is God's unique message to us, the Bible.

God's Word is noted as being "living and effective and sharper than any double-edged sword" (Hebrews

4:12, CSB). And in the second book of Timothy, the Scriptures are described as being useful for: (1) teaching what is true, (2) correcting our mistakes, (3) making our lives whole again, and (4) training us to do what is right (2 Timothy 3:16, NIRV). What more could we possibly need?

For centuries, countless lives have been changed by the gospel message of the Bible—the message of Jesus being crucified, dying, and then resurrected to life. By Jesus conquering death and sin, we have been offered the free gift of eternal life in the family of God. And this powerful gift is available to all of us, regardless of our past, present, or even our future.

Hebrews 13:8 assures us: "Jesus Christ is the same yesterday, today, and forever" (CSB). The world will change. Technology will change. And you and I will certainly change. What a comfort to know that we can count on Jesus to remain the same! His power and love for us will never be outdated. And that my friend is a timeless truth.

By using Scripture, the servant of God can be completely prepared to do every good thing.   2 TIMOTHY 3:17 (NIRV)

Think it Through: In what area of your life do you struggle most to utilize God's Word? Teaching what is true? Correcting your mistakes? Making your life whole? Training to do what is right? (see 2 Timothy 3:16)

Make it Personal: Lord, I want to experience the full power and value of Your Word in my life. Today, I will use Your Word to:

_____

_____

_____

_____

_____

Day 22

Same Old Sunday Dinner

*N*ine-year-old Naomi asked that inevitable question of the day no mom can escape: *"What's for dinner?"* I gave her a run-down of the menu for that Sunday: baked chicken, collard greens, sweet potatoes, brown rice, and cornbread. A reply from my child such as "okay great" or "thanks mom" would have been nice. Instead she added, "Why do we always have the *same thing* for Sunday dinner? Did Jesus eat a lot of chicken?"

Perhaps that was my mommy-cue to remind my daughter she should be grateful just to have food! However I had to admit, Naomi had a point. Out of routine, I *do* tend to cook just about the same dinner Sunday after Sunday. It's like clock-work for me to prepare those particular dishes, and I need as much routine in my life as possible to keep my sanity. Can I get an "amen"?

Preparing the same menu Sunday after Sunday certainly isn't the crime of the century. But falling into autopilot mode as we walk out our daily relationships with God can be more harmful than it may seem. For instance, do we pray before meals just because we're accustomed to doing so? Or are we truly thinking about how grateful we are to have such an abundance to eat? Do we read a Scripture a day to keep the devil away? Or are we desperate to spend time with the One who loves us most? Do we press our way to church just because it's the Sunday event for the day? Or are we sincerely eager to worship God with fellow believers?

There is certainly a profitable place for routine and discipline in life. Yet if we're just going through the motions of spiritual activities, our relationships with God don't grow. God is interested in our hearts and minds, not mere performance out of habit or familiarity.

God keeps His relationship with us fresh. The daily bread He gives us is not stale (Matthew 6:11), and He gives us new mercies every morning (Lamentations 3:22). So spend some time today thinking of how you can re-engage your heart in your daily time with God, your mealtime, or your morning or evening prayers. Ask your kids for suggestions! They always have creative ideas.

In the meantime, I guess I better come up with another Sunday dinner menu. Naomi eagerly offered me her biblical suggestions:

We should have fish and bread like the 5000 people had, grape juice since Jesus turned water into wine, and apples since they were probably in the Garden of Eden. Wait! Was that the fruit they weren't supposed to eat?

Because of the Lord's faithful love we do not perish, for his mercies never end. They are new every morning; great is your faithfulness!   LAMENTATIONS 3:22-23 (CSB)

Think it Through: Identify one thing you often do out of routine in your relationship with God, with no real passion or purpose: _____
Think of how you can re-engage your heart into what has become monotonous, familiar, or meaningless. Now, change it up! Share your idea with a friend.

Make it Personal: Lord, help me fully engage my heart and mind with You each day. Despite the routine of life, help me pursue You with passion. I want my relationship with You to be vibrant, intentional, and full of purpose.

When I become complacent, jog my memory that You give me new mercies every morning.

_____

_____

_____

_____

_____

Day 23

❧

Selling Out

Click-click-click. Click-click-click. Our gas stovetop wasn't lighting as easily as it should, hence that annoying clicking sound from the burner. Turning the dial once more, 12-year-old Karis was determined to boil pasta. She finally got the stovetop to light, but in the process, flames abruptly sparked up around the sides of the pot.

Naomi, age 10 at the time, had always been terribly afraid of flames, matches, or any other item even remotely related to fire. She'd morph into a state of extreme caution or panic, and this situation was no exception.

"Karis!" scolded Naomi, "*Be careful.* You could burn your hand off!" With sincere concern in her voice Naomi continued, "Or worse, the whole stove could blow up and you might get killed!"

Even though it was a bit dramatic, I thought Naomi's display of care for her sister's well-being was quite touching. Too bad it was short-lived. Seemingly right in her next breath, Naomi quickly added, "And if you die, can I have your room, your money, and all your other stuff?"

Unbelievable! So much for genuine sisterly concern. Naomi became distracted by the possibility of gaining a few coveted items and "sold out" her sister within seconds.

I'm ashamed to admit that sometimes I sell out my Heavenly Father. It's never intentional, and I always seem to have a good excuse at the time . . . but it's really just that, an excuse. Can anyone relate? We say we value our relationship with God over everything, but sometimes the ways we invest our time, talent, and treasure prove otherwise. Yes, we simply sell out, pushing aside the principles of God's Word that we otherwise say we value.

We're committed to spending time with God each morning until we hit that snooze button to sleep in a little more. We avoid gossip until we decide to "share a prayer concern" about someone's child. We extol the virtues of truth and honesty until we tell a "white lie" or exaggerate to avoid embarrassment. We make plans to volunteer until something "more important" demands our time. Or we have to pray about donating to that worthy cause, but we'll order those must-have shoes online without a second thought.

Sadly, I'm guilty of all those things. Thankfully God forgives us when we confess, and I've had to do a great deal of confessing in this area. If we don't intentionally develop a sincere attitude of honoring God with our day to day choices, it hinders our growth in Him. It also damages our relationships with others.

This is a tough one, and our gracious Father certainly does not expect us to be perfect in all our ways. However, whether it's hard or easy; to our gain or our loss; convenient or inconvenient—don't sell out! Stand committed to what God values and the principles of His Word. If we must sell out for something, let's be sold out to the cause of Christ and His kingdom.

For me, to live is Christ and to die is gain.

PHILIPPIANS 1:21 (CSB)

For where your treasure is, there your heart will be also.

MATTHEW 6:21 (CSB)

Think it Through: When are you most tempted to sell out the values or principles of God's Word? What area of your life needs greater integrity to help you better represent the kingdom of God? What beliefs or attitudes do you need to lay before God to transform for His glory?

Make it Personal: Lord, help me rely on the supernatural power of the Holy Spirit to honor You with my daily choices, moment by moment. Give me the strength to stand strong when I am tempted to compromise or place my personal gain or comfort before You and Your kingdom. I need Your power to have greater integrity in the area of:

_____

_____

_____

_____

_____

Day 24

Grace at the Checkout Counter

$\mathcal{I}$ must come across as the meanest mom in the world when I shop with my children. If they ask for candy, toys, or any other trinket at a checkout counter, *very rarely* do I purchase them anything. Yet despite my sincere efforts to deter my children from impulse buying, there is obviously some type of conspiracy working against me. I can remember at least four times when—for reasons I will never understand—various customers actually *gave* my daughters money to purchase random items in the checkout line. Yes, these patrons joyfully handed over to my children what I had assumed was hard-earned cash. Though the amount may have been a couple of dollars at most, I'd still be thinking, *"Why are these people giving my children money? They haven't done anything to deserve it!"*

On one occasion, a *cashier* actually purchased those 99-cents cartons of Goldfish crackers for my seven and nine-year-olds. I will admit, my kids had voluntarily stacked up a few of those hand-held shopping baskets. Nevertheless, I couldn't help but think, *"All they did was clean up a few baskets. I just don't get it."*

As I stewed in our minivan contemplating whether or not my daughters were worthy of Goldfish crackers, I suddenly felt convicted. Why was I making such a big deal about my children receiving something I felt they didn't deserve, yet I didn't pay for? Hasn't God done the same for me?

Do I deserve salvation? Absolutely not. Yet God has freely given me eternal life by His grace. Do I deserve the never-ending love of God? Not based on some of my thoughts and actions! Yet God continues to grace me with His unconditional love.

Doesn't God continuously grant grace every day that protects, forgives, and provides for us? Simply because He is a kind and compassionate God, He covers us with grace—even though we certainly don't deserve it.

I've concluded it's wise for me to refrain from judging who deserves grace, or when and how grace should be granted. Instead, I should be thankful that I receive abundant grace every day. In turn, I should grant that same grace to others as freely as God gives it to me.

God is full of grace. From him we have all received grace . . . grace and truth come to us through Jesus Christ.

JOHN 1:16-17 (NIrV)

Think it Through: How can you grant grace to someone in your life (husband, child, family member, co-worker, boss, friend, neighbor)? Be specific and do it.

Make it Personal: Lord, help me freely extend grace to others from day to day, especially in light of the grace You have shown and continue to give me each day. Today I can show grace by:

_____

_____

_____

_____

_____

Day 25

Excuses, Excuses

One thing children certainly do *not* lack is creativity. When it comes to making excuses or offering explanations, their perspectives can be quite inventive. Consider the six-year-old son of my friend Teresa. She found him visibly upset one afternoon and upon asking why he was crying, her son tearfully replied, "I'm not crying. My eyes are just sweating."

Or take my 13-year-old niece. One day her mom remarked that the teen's bedroom looked like it had been hit by a tornado *and* a cyclone. My niece calmly responded, "My room is not a mess. Everything is just on display."

Both of these kids get major points for innovative thinking!

Sometimes as parents, we don't do much better than our children when it comes to rationalizing our actions. We justify yelling at our kids with the proverbial, "You are getting on my *last* nerve!" Or instead of admitting to our children that we did something wrong, we go on and on with explanations for *why* we did *what* we did . . . *blah, blah, blah.*

Excuses-in-disguise tend to fall somewhere between denial, pride, stubbornness, and fooling ourselves. Coming clean by admitting our mistakes, shortcomings, and faults can certainly be humbling and embarrassing, but it's absolutely necessary. Confessing sin is key in our relationships with God and our children. Kids have already figured out that we are less than perfect parents, so there is no point in trying to keep up that charade. Modeling how to acknowledge our wrongs and apologize is one of the greatest gifts we can give our children.

Fighting the tendency to make excuses is challenging, and we may not win every battle. But if we simply own up to the times we mess up, we demonstrate to our children the best way to repair our relationships with God and others.

It's time to come clean with God, ourselves, and our children. No more excuses.

Therefore confess your sins to each other and pray for each other so that you may be healed. The prayer of a righteous person is powerful and effective. JAMES 5:16 (NIV)

Think it Through: Do you need to confess and apologize to your child, spouse, or anyone else for something you've done that you are hesitant to admit? Commit to a time and place you will go to that person and confess. Pray about what God would have you say. Be sure to express that you were wrong and ask for forgiveness.

Make it Personal: Lord, it's so hard to simply confess when I'm wrong, but I know I need to. Help me to quickly admit wrongdoing and not make excuses. Let me humbly ask for Your forgiveness and forgiveness from others. Today, I confess:

_____

_____

_____

_____

_____

Day 26

❧

Spelling
Word Shortcut

The fourth-grade teacher's mandate was clear: *All spelling word sentences must contain at least 11 words.* Ten-year-old Naomi was not the least bit enthused about this new rule. I, on the other hand, had high hopes this requirement would encourage her to abandon writing "baby sentences" and move towards incorporating more thoughtful and complex phrases. She needed that challenge, and I was glad someone besides me would be pushing her to mature in her writing.

And so the spelling-words sulking began! My daughter would plop into her daily homework spot and often become frustrated with writing the required eleven-word sentences. One afternoon Naomi begged for help with creating a sentence for the word *apprehension*. I gave her some general hints, but I ultimately compelled her to compose the sentence on her own. Sighing heavily, Naomi trudged back to her homework spot, dismayed that I didn't outright provide her with a sentence.

Later that evening, I spotted Naomi's homework folder on top of her school backpack. Curious as to how she completed the spelling sentence, I found the assignment and read the following: "*Writing a sentence for the word apprehension is very, very, very, very, very, very hard.*"

Only Naomi! I should have known that particular child would find a way to circumnavigate the purpose of the eleven-word standard, yet technically meet the requirement.

The next morning I confronted my daughter about her "sentence." She had the audacity to reply, "Well, what's wrong with it? It *is* a sentence! And it even has *15* words."

I could see right through my daughter's pseudo-effort to write that sentence. And sometimes, I'm just as guilty of half-hearted compliance in my relationship with God. Have you been there? You sense God's prompting to do or say something in particular, but you just won't bring yourself to outright obey. It might be sharing the gospel with a co-worker, or giving to a family in need. It could be apologizing to your spouse, or taking time to listen to your child when you're busy. Instead of simply doing exactly what God asks, we stall or partially comply. Even worse, we finagle a way to obey the letter of the law, but not the spirit of what God is leading us to do.

Our Father continually orchestrates opportunities to stretch our faith in Him. When we take the seemingly easy way out through feigned obedience, we forfeit the growth God intended for us. He is trying to move us away from the "baby stuff" and move us towards spiritual maturity. We often stunt our spiritual growth and end up still having to face similar obedience hurdles in the future. Yet even when we don't fully obey, God continues to love us and give us grace and mercy. He gives us chance after chance to practice obedience and learn to trust Him more.

The next time you are tempted to disregard God's leading or dress up half-effort as sincere obedience, remember that the only person you are fooling is yourself. Instead, take a moment to pray and rely on the power of the Holy Spirit to help you choose to obey. Then try again with a fully willing spirit, committed to following our gracious Heavenly Father.

Jesus replied, "But even more blessed are all who hear the word of God and put it into practice." LUKE 11:28 (NLT)

Therefore let us move beyond the elementary teachings about Christ and be taken forward to maturity.

HEBREWS 6:1A (NIV)

Think it Through: In what area of your life do you struggle with full obedience to God? What roadblock is keeping you from spiritual maturity? Ask God to show you an area if one doesn't come to mind immediately. Write a Scripture addressing that issue on an index card or sticky note. Memorize and focus on that Scripture this week in your time with God.

Make it Personal: Lord, I confess disobedience in my life. Show me the ways I am limiting my spiritual growth. Give me a heart to repent and fully do Your will. Thank you for giving me opportunities to grow in You through obedience. I especially desire to fully obey You in the area of:

_____

_____

_____

_____

_____

Day 27

Not So Easy

*E*ver heard the phrase *"It's as easy as taking candy from a baby"*? Usually this expression implies that a somewhat devious plan will be quite simple to accomplish, no matter who or what might be involved with the task. Well, eight-year-old Joy didn't quite see it that way. This was her assessment:

> *Taking candy from a baby isn't easy. First, you have to find a baby. Then, you have to find a baby with candy. Then you have to take the candy from the baby. Then, the baby might cry. And then, the mama will get mad at you for taking candy from her baby. So that's really not "easy".*

Wow! From Joy's perspective, taking candy from a baby could actually turn out to be quite complicated. In fact, it might result in the unintended consequences of a crying baby and a furious mom. You could land in a sticky situation that suddenly isn't worth the candy you thought would be so easy to take.

Unfortunately, selfish choices that seem harmless at the time can also leave us with unintended consequences. Sometimes we only think through our choices to the point of what we *intend* to happen or *think* will happen. But the consequences of self-centered actions can be more far-reaching than we could ever imagine. Our choices indeed impact the people around us, for better or for worse.

Self-serving decisions can also lead to facing natural consequences that sting. Consequences have a unique way of disciplining us, yet simultaneously give us the opportunity to make wiser decisions in the future. Proverbs 3:11 encourages us not to despise God's discipline. His loving purpose in discipline is to mold us into becoming more and more like Christ.

The next time you're tempted to make a selfish decision that you think won't hurt anyone, think again. You just might end up in a situation that is far from easy. Though we will experience discipline from our

Heavenly Father, we can confess and repent from our wrongdoing. God is not only faithful to discipline us, but He is faithful to forgive us time after time. What a gracious and loving Father we serve!

No discipline seems pleasant at the time, but painful. Later on, however, it produces a harvest of righteousness and peace for those who have been trained by it.

HEBREWS 12:11 (NIV)

My child, don't reject the Lord's discipline, and don't be upset when he corrects you. For the Lord corrects those he loves. PROVERBS 3:11–12A (NLT)

Think it Through: What self-centered choice have you made that caused painful consequences to yourself or someone else: _____

If you haven't already, confess that choice as sin and determine a wiser choice you can make now that will honor God.

What possible future situation can you foresee in which you might be tempted to make a quick, selfish decision? Pray now and ask God for wisdom to make a different decision in line with His will.

Make it Personal: Lord, thank You for loving me enough to discipline me when I am outside of Your will. Help me consider others before making thoughtless or selfish choices. When I stumble in this area, help me to simply confess my sin and not make excuses. I want to learn quickly from consequences so that I can move forward in my journey with You.

_____

_____

_____

_____

_____

Day 28

Computers for Dummies

*O*ne afternoon I was enjoying a radio segment while running errands in my minivan. The host was taking phone calls from parents with funny stories about their children. A dad called in and shared the following:

> *I was in a bookstore with my eight-year-old son. We were standing in line and he pointed to a book and asked, "Is the name of that book really Computers for Dummies?" I looked at the title and answered, "Yep, that's really the name, Computers for Dummies." Then my son said, "And people still buy it?"*

Pretty insightful for an eight-year-old! In his mind, why would you be willing to *pay* to take instruction from something or someone calling you a dummy?

Paying for a book that calls me a "dummy" is one thing. But paying attention to the voice of the enemy is a different matter. I wish I could say I'm always wise enough to ignore that sly voice of deception, but that certainly wouldn't be a true statement. In fact, falling for the tricks of the enemy has been around since . . . Genesis.

The enemy knows exactly what tempts us the most or easily causes us to compromise. He knows our weaknesses, fears, and struggles, and his goal is to take our focus off God. It's like the enemy is saying, *"Dummy, come here!"* or *"Dummy, go over there!"* and we keep falling for it. Red flags and caution signs are all over the place. Yet we keep heading towards the trap instead of seeking the Holy Spirit for strength to overcome the enemy.

God's Word gives us several strategies to avoid pitfalls the enemy has planned for us:
- *resisting (James 4:7)*
- *fleeing (1 Corinthians 6:18)*
- *putting on spiritual armor (Ephesians 6:11)*
- *meditating on Scripture (Psalm 1:2)*
- *being accountable to others (Galatians 6:1-2)*

These are just a few of the highly effective tactical approaches at our disposal. Choosing to remain easy prey and open targets for the enemy's darts is a losing strategy. And I don't know about you, but I am not trying to lose.

The only book that can keep us from falling for the enemy's schemes is God's foolproof manual for victorious living: the Bible. We can outsmart the enemy by consistently applying the Word of God to our lives each day. Engage in the battle! It's worth the fight.

Be alert and of sober mind. Your enemy the devil prowls around like a roaring lion looking for someone to devour.

1 PETER 5:8 (NIV)

Think it Through: What temptation do you all too often fall for? Identify a biblical strategy you can use to fight that temptation effectively. Write out a Scripture supporting that strategy, and meditate on it until you memorize it. Recite the Scripture whenever that particular temptation comes.

Make it Personal: Lord, help me to be wise about the schemes of the enemy. Let me not fight in my own power, but instead stand on Your Word and practice biblical strategies under the power of the Holy Spirit. Today, I will begin memorizing the Scripture:

OUT OF THE MOUTHS OF BABES

_____

_____

_____

_____

_____

_____

_____

Day 29

Plank Removal in Progress

I could hear the tension building as I washed dishes in the kitchen sink. With my hands dripping wet, I quickly made my way into the family room to assess the situation. Six-year-old Joy was trying desperately (to no avail) to beat her sister Naomi in Wii game after Wii game.

"I messed up again!" Joy complained in frustration, "It's not fair. I never win."

In an attempt to console the sore loser, I noted, "That's not true Joy. I've seen you win plenty of video games. You can't expect to win *every* game. Nobody's perfect."

Thinking of my oldest daughter I added, "Karis usually beats all of us when she plays Wii, but does she play every game perfectly?"

Still pouting and not wanting to answer, Joy sat in silence. Eight-year-old Naomi was happy to answer for her sister, and she sweetly chimed, "*No-o-o-o.*"

To drive my point home further, I decided to reference each member of our family. "Does *Daddy* get everything right all of the time?" I asked. Joy continued her silence, so I waited for Naomi to back me up. Once again, Naomi answered in a sing-song voice, "*No-o-o-o.*"

I went on, "Does *Mommy* do everything perfectly?" My supportive back-up suddenly altered her sweet, loving tone and emphatically declared, "Oh definitely not *you* Mommy! You mess up all the time."

Glaring at Naomi, I cleverly asked, "What about *Naomi*?" Both Joy and I turned to Naomi to await her response. After a few seconds, Naomi confidently smirked, "Well, of course *I'm* perfect because I'm just awesome like that!"

Why is it so incredibly easy—even satisfying—to identify imperfections in others, yet ignore our own inadequacies? Many times I have been quick to highlight what I view as flaws in my children, even with an air of condemnation or judgment. Perhaps that's why

Matthew 7:1-5 is so sobering. It warns us to take the big plank of wood out of our own eye before complaining about the little speck of dust in someone else's eye.

Scolding and criticizing our children without being mindful of our own shortcomings is a tricky blind spot. Yes, it's our job to train, correct, and discipline our children when necessary. But sometimes we parent with a tone and attitude of arrogance, implying that we *never* make mistakes. And let's face it, that strategy doesn't work. Our children see straight through that façade. Parenting from a place of "let me check myself first" can be much more effective. And if we also apologize when we make mistakes, that further models humility to our children.

As parents who are indeed human, we have our share of flaws and issues, so let's just own it. Spend some time today examining the two-by-four block of wood in your own eye. The trace of sawdust in your child's eye can wait—at least for 24 hours.

How can you say to your brother, "Let me take the speck out of your eye," when all the time there is a plank in your own eye? MATTHEW 7:4 (NIV)

Think it Through: Think of an instance when you were overly critical of your child. Confess it to God in prayer and apologize to your child.

Make it Personal: Lord, help me not to be so critical of my children. Teach me to admonish and guide them in loving, healthy ways. Help me set an example of accepting and admitting my own imperfections. Today, I confess my tendency to criticize _____ (child) about _____ .
Help me examine myself before being quick to judge.

_____

_____

_____

_____

_____

Day 30

Spam

$\mathcal{S}$pam. Another word like *mouse* and *tablet* that can have a totally different meaning depending on when you were born. While grocery shopping with my children in tow, eleven-year-old Naomi noticed a can of *SPAM* lunch meat on the shelf. Pointing to the bright yellow capital letters on the classic blue wrapper, she declared with pity, "That's just *sad*. They actually make a food called SPAM. Nobody likes spam emails! People don't even read it. Why would they name it SPAM if they really want people to buy it?"

Though Naomi was applying 21st-century technology jargon to a product made famous from World

War II, she had pretty good marketing insight for an eleven-year-old. If the idea is to convince consumers to buy a product, perhaps the packaging shouldn't display a name that automatically brings a negative connotation to mind. In fact, the outside packaging should draw customers to consider the product, not push a potential buyer away. Certainly the name of a product should represent it well, not convey that it is bothersome and not even worth considering.

My daughter's comment got me thinking . . . how well does my "packaging" represent Jesus? Are my countenance, demeanor, and words more likely to draw someone towards wanting to know more about Christ? Or am I more likely to cause someone to quickly delete the whole notion like Spam-mail?

No one can reflect Jesus perfectly here on this earth—that's not what God requires of us. However, there are times we all too easily fall victim to anger, pride, greed, selfishness, lack of compassion, or rudeness. All of these certainly don't represent the kingdom of God very well.

If we want others to be drawn to our Savior, we can start by developing and displaying the fruit of the Spirit in our lives: love, joy, peace, patience, kindness, goodness, gentleness, faithfulness, and self-control (Galatians

5:22-23). One of the best ways we witness to the world is through how we treat others. God's Word reminds us that the way people will know we are His followers is by how we show love to others (John 13:34-35). It's true; *you* might be the only Jesus someone will ever see or experience.

As His children, God calls us to the great honor of being ambassadors for His kingdom (2 Corinthians 5:20). To represent Christ well, we must rely on the power of the Holy Spirit moment by moment. And that, my friends, is a challenge! Romans 12:1 charges us to be a "living sacrifice." Think about how painful that is—to be *living* while being *sacrificed.* Excruciatingly painful, but necessary.

When we operate in our selfish nature, it's impossible to display the fruit of the Spirit in our lives. But by relying on the power of God, we can show Christ's love to others and represent His kingdom well.

Therefore, we are ambassadors for Christ, since God is making his appeal through us. 2 CORINTHIANS 5:20A (CSB)

Therefore, I urge you, brothers and sisters, in view of God's mercy, to offer your bodies as a living sacrifice, holy and pleasing to God—this is your true and proper worship.

ROMANS 12:1 (NIV)

Think it Through: Are you conscious of being an ambassador for the kingdom of Heaven? In what situations are you more likely to behave in ways that reflect Christ poorly? To represent Christ better, which trait in the fruit of the Spirit do you most need to further develop in your life?

Make it Personal: Lord, help me view my role of being an ambassador for Your kingdom as a great honor and my first priority. Help me practice obedience to the Holy Spirit to display the *fruit of the Spirit* more consistently in my life. In particular, help me to develop (*love, joy, peace, patience, kindness, goodness, gentleness, faithfulness, self-control* - Galatians 5:22-23):

_____

_____

_____

_____

_____

Day 31

The Simplicity of Salvation

$\mathcal{I}$'m incredibly grateful that all three of my children made choices to follow Jesus at young ages. My oldest accepted Christ when she was five years old. She had a bedtime conversation with her dad about what it meant to be in the family of God. The next morning, she prayed and asked Jesus to come into her heart. She told me the news later, and I was elated that she had chosen to make Jesus her Lord and Savior! However, I must admit I felt a hint of disappointment because I wasn't present when she made the most important decision she'd ever make in her life. I later comforted myself with the thought that I had two more children, thus two more chances, to have that "moment" as a mom.

A few years later, I had a prime opportunity to share the gospel with my seven-year-old middle child. She listened intently and then politely announced that she preferred to wait until she was eight years old to make the commitment to follow Christ. *What?* She had no particular reason for wanting to delay this monumental decision, and I was a bit perturbed that she wasn't making the choice with me right then and there. I mean, this was the chance I had been waiting for, and she was dashing my dream!

A few weeks later (before turning eight I might add), this same child asked Jesus to become her Savior at school after reading a children's booklet about joining the family of God. Once again, I missed the moment.

I now had only one more child and one more chance to witness at least one of my offspring making her initial decision to follow Christ. When my youngest child Joy was four, she directly asked me how a person goes to Heaven. I could hardly contain myself! Finally, I was getting the moment I'd been longing for.

I proceeded to answer her question with what I planned to be a masterful presentation of the gospel to a four-year-old. About 20 seconds into my soliloquy, Joy interrupted with, "God, I am very, very, very, very, very, very sorry for all of the things I've done wrong. Please forgive me."

Dumbfounded, I quickly shut my mouth and realized the miracle I was experiencing right before my eyes . . . the miracle I almost talked right through being full of my own desires as a mother. I watched as my daughter simplified what I was making way more complex than it needed to be. One more lesson the child taught the mom.

I should have taken the hint from the apostle Paul who insightfully declares in 1 Corinthians 1:17b:

> *He commanded me not to preach with wisdom and fancy words. That would take all the power away from the cross of Christ.* (NIRV)

If you haven't invited Jesus into your life to be your Savior and Lord, a simple heartfelt prayer will do. Fancy jargon isn't necessary, but a humble spirit realizing a need for a Savior is a must. Once you make that life-changing decision, reading and absorbing God's love letter to you (the Bible) becomes the key to growing in your new relationship with Him.

My fellow moms, I truly hope you embrace both the challenges and joys of the parenting journey with your children. But my ultimate prayer is for you to experience a *personal* journey with God through Jesus Christ. If you have already started that journey, share the hope you have in Jesus with another mom. She just might need a little encouragement to make it through one more day.

If you confess with your mouth, "Jesus is Lord," and believe in your heart that God raised him from the dead, you will be saved . . . For everyone who calls on the name of the Lord will be saved. ROMANS 10:9-13 (CSB)

Think it Through: Have you made a decision to follow Jesus as your Savior and Lord? Have you strayed away from your walk with Him? Do you need to recommit your life to Him?

Is there someone you need to tell about Jesus? Who might that person be: _____

Make it Personal: God, I realize I need You. I confess my sin before You. Thank you for sending Your Son Jesus to pay the price for my sins by dying on a cross and rising from the dead. Come into my heart and be my Savior and Lord. I want to follow you all the days of my life. I commit myself to You as a decision of my will on this day, (date) _____ . Amen.

_____

_____

_____

_____

_____

If you made the commitment today to begin a relationship with Jesus Christ, or to recommit your life to Him, I'd love to encourage you more at:

www.yourmommymoments.com.

Will You Take the Mommy-Moments Challenge?

You did it mom! You completed this devotional of 31 stories revealing how everyday interactions with children can lead to lessons and insights from God. So now, will you take the challenge I presented in the introduction of this book? The challenge to listen to your children with a different ear?

I cannot encourage you enough to make note of memorable conversations and exchanges with your children. Briefly scribble them on a piece of paper or in a journal, type them in your cell phone notes, or start a folder on your laptop—whatever works for you. Your experiences might be humorous, disheartening, joy-filled, or challenging. Even if a revelation from above doesn't stand out in the moment, God may reveal a personal message at a later time . . . and I promise, you don't want to miss it.

Share your mommy-moments with Nicole at:
www.yourmommymoments.com

Encouragement for the Journey

I've experienced some incredibly great mommy-moments, many of which I treasure and shared with you in the pages of this devotional. But the reality any mom can attest to is that motherhood also comes with some not so good times. Some flat-out bad times. Some difficult and challenging times. And one hurdle I never expected to face was postpartum depression. Yet it was indeed part of my journey, as it is for 1 in 7 new mothers.

I remember in my darkest hour feeling like I wanted to go away . . . just escape to a place where *something* could fix the broken me. Or perhaps take a very long nap and *somehow* wake up no longer feeling like I was walking underwater, through quicksand, with a blindfold on and one hand tied behind my back. Oh, how I desperately wanted to be free from the crippling anxiety and the thick, overwhelming fog that was causing my brain to function so slowly. Every task took at least twice as long, if not longer. I was living in super-slow motion in a place that was familiar, yet somehow strangely foreign. My brain was refusing to cooperate with my life, no matter how hard I tried and prayed.

So I wanted to go away to get better. But first, I wanted to freeze-frame my family. I didn't want one day to go by. I wanted to return from my escape or wake up from my slumber at exactly the same point in time as when I had left. I didn't want to miss *anything*; I just wanted to be me again.

My faith was a much-needed source of hope during my journey through postpartum depression, as well as in my recovery and healing process. After finally accepting treatment and support, my perspective of my postpartum experience slowly started to change over time. I had initially felt that my season of depression was a total waste of time. I clearly remember commenting to God: "Seriously, You could have just skipped that part of my life because there was absolutely no purpose in it *whatsoever*." In my mind, invaluable time to enjoy my life and children had been stolen from me. I would never get that time back, and I was outright mad.

But to my surprise, I eventually began to see purpose in my struggle. I started believing that "what the enemy meant for evil, God meant for good" (Genesis 50:20). I gained newfound determination. I was not going to allow the most difficult season of my life to deny me the joys of being a mom. Embracing the everyday moments with my children was my way of taking my life back, and it worked.

I found a new confidence in God's ability to help me weather any other storms that would surely come my way as a mom. I just needed to stay the course and hold on tight to His hand. And along the way, I could support and encourage other mothers through their storms. I could do that with greater empathy and insight than I ever could before.

Postpartum depression may not be part of your story. But on your motherhood journey, there will be unforeseen challenges, daily distractions, life responsibilities, unexpected hardships, and complicated circumstances beyond your control. My prayer for you is that *despite* any of these experiences, please don't resent or miss anything on your unique journey of being a mom. The joys and challenges both have purpose and can draw you closer to God in ways you could never imagine. With

Him you will find strength to endure the storms and savor the joys. *Slow down* . . . take in every God-moment He gives you through your children. I promise, you won't be disappointed.

⌐

Connect with Nicole at:
www.yourmommymoments.com

CPSIA information can be obtained
at www.ICGtesting.com
Printed in the USA
BVHW080741140521
607270BV00005B/588